From Me To YOU

HANDMADE GIFTS FOR YOUR VIP

by Mari Bolte

CAPSTONE PRESS
a capstone imprint

Snap Books are published by Capstone Press,
1710 Roe Crest Drive, North Mankato, Minnesota 56003
www.capstonepub.com

Library of Congress Cataloging-in-Publication Data

Bolte, Mari, author.
From me to you : handmade gifts for your VIPs /
by Mari Bolte.
pages cm. — (Snap books. Make it, gift it.)
Summary: "Step-by-step instructions, tips, and
full-color photographs will help teens and tweens create
personalized presents"—Provided by publisher.
Audience: Ages 9–12.
Audience: Grades 4 to 6.
ISBN 978-1-4914-5201-1 (library binding)
ISBN 978-1-4914-5217-2 (paperback)
ISBN 978-1-4914-5217-2 (eBook PDF)

1. Handicraft—Juvenile literature. 2. Gifts—Juvenile
literature. I. Title.

TT160.B6525 2016
745.5—dc23   2015015948

Designer: Tracy Davies McCabe
Craft Project Creator: Marcy Morin
Photo Stylist: Sarah Schuette
Production Specialist: Laura Manthe

Photo Credits:
All photos by Capstone Press: Karon Dubke

Artistic Effects:
shutterstock

Printed in the United States of America in
North Mankato, Minnesota.
052015 008823CGF15

Table of CONTENTS

Very Important Presents   4

Send-worthy Stationery   6

Pooch Plaque   8

Shine Bright Centerpiece   10

Prop Block   12

Sugary Snow Globes   14

Memory Box   18

Curious Candy   20

Totally Taped   22

Style Statement   24

Fold It, Hold It   26

Tick Tock   28

Memorable Mittens   30

Read More   32

Very Important Presents

The very important people in your life deserve top-shelf gifts. Customize each project to each person's likes and personalities and show them they really are your VIPs.

Simply Wrapped

What You'll Need:

gift in a box

wrapping paper

clear tape

ribbon

1. Remove any tags or labels from your gift. (Especially the price tag!)
2. Measure the wrapping paper. It should be wide enough to overlap a litle when folded over the gift. The sides should overlap slightly when folded toward each other.
3. Center the gift upside down on the wrapping paper. Wrap the paper around the gift and gently pull until tight. The wrapping paper should overlap in the center of the gift. Secure with tape.
4. On one side of the package, fold the ends of the wrapping paper toward each other. Firmly crease around the box's edges. Crease the triangle-shaped flaps. Repeat on the other side of the package.

5. Fold down the top flap, creasing the top edge. Fold up the bottom flap, creasing at the bottom edge. Secure with tape.
6. Pinch two fingers together and run them along every edge of the gift. This will create a crisp fold.
7. Finish your gift with a ribbon. Cut the ends of the ribbon at an angle for a prettier presentation.

CRAFTING TIPS:

Use heavy-duty wrapping paper. It makes sharper creases and won't rip or tear as easily as thinner paper. Double-sided tape will give your package a clean appearance too.

If the seam at the bottom of the package bothers you, measure the wrapping paper so it's 1½ times longer than your package. That way, the edge of the wrapping paper will line up with the edge of the gift.

Use the ribbon to tie in decorative trinkets. A few ideas include ornaments, extra-large Christmas lights, faux flowers, and feathers. Use a mini whisk or spatula for a kitchen VIP. Cinnamon sticks, candy canes, and small pine branches will make your gift smell sweet. Sleigh bells will help your present both look and sound festive.

Send-worthy Stationery

Giving personalized stationery means thank-you notes just got a whole lot more fun!

Notecards:

What You'll Need:

hot glue gun

blank notecards

used dryer sheet

pigment ink pen (or other pen with slow-drying ink)

embossing powder

1. Plug in the glue gun so it can preheat.
2. Wipe the notecard with the dryer sheet. The sheet will reduce the amount of static on the card and give you a cleaner finished look.
3. Write your word across the card. Quickly sprinkle embossing powder over the wet ink.
4. Tap off any excess embossing powder. Use a small paintbrush to dust off any specks that remain.
5. Hold the metal tip of the glue gun as close to the embossing powder as possible. The heat from the glue gun should melt the powder. Move the glue gun across the card's surface until the embossing powder is melted and raised.

Lined Envelopes:

What You'll Need:

envelope

gift wrap

double-sided tape

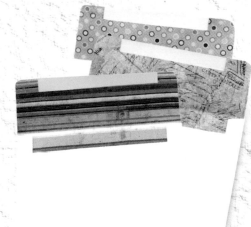

1. Open the envelope. Trace the envelope's shape on the back side of the gift wrap.
2. Cut out the envelope tracing about ¼ inch (0.6 centimeter) inside the traced line. Cut off the bottom ½ inch (1.2 cm) of the liner.
3. Slide the liner inside the envelope with the printed side up. Secure it with double-sided tape.

Pooch Plaque

The perfect gift for your pet-loving VIP—and their Very Important Pet! Tweak the message to fit your recipient's personality, and add as many hooks as you need.

What You'll Need:

picture

wooden plaque

chalk

acrylic paint and paintbrush

metal hook with screws

CRAFTING TIPS:

TURN THIS INTO A JEWELRY OR KEY RING HOLDER FOR THE PETLESS PERSON.

INSTEAD OF A PLAIN HOOK, USE METAL HOOKS, WOOD HANGERS, OR HARDWARE FOR CABINETS.

1. Print out your picture and desired message. Trim the paper to fit on the piece of wood.
2. Color the entire back of the paper with chalk. Flip the paper over and place on the wood. Tape it into place.
3. Use a pencil to trace the picture and letters. Work in sections to avoid smearing the chalk as you trace.
4. Once your letters have transferred to the wood, you can paint them.
5. Once your first section is dry, you can trace and paint the next piece. Continue until your entire picture and message are painted. Let the entire sign dry completely.
6. Screw in the metal coat hook.

Shine Bright Centerpiece

This shimmering centerpiece will both brighten someone's day and reflect well on your friendship.

For the Tea Lights

What You'll Need:

blue glitter

silver glitter

white glue

foam brush

three glass tea light holders

1. Divide glitter into three small bowls:
   bowl 1—all blue glitter
   bowl 2—all silver glitter
   bowl 3—1 part blue glitter, 1 part silver glitter
2. Thin the glue with water so it's spreadable, about 3 parts glue to 1 part water. Brush glue inside the bottom half of a tea light holder.
3. Pour some of the glitter from bowl 1 into the tea light holder. Rotate the tea light holder until all the glue is covered in glitter. Tap out excess glitter. Set tea light holder aside to dry.
4. Repeat steps 2–3 with the remaining glitter and tea light holders.

For the Mirrors

What You'll Need:

paper doily

tape

mirror

frosted glass spray paint

1. Lay the doily over the mirror. When it's positioned how you want it, wrap the back edges around the mirror and tape in place.
2. Spray a coat of frosted glass spray paint over the mirror. Let dry completely, at least 5 minutes or according to the instructions on the can.
3. Remove the tape and doily.

Prop Block

Both the classic cookbook chef and the modern-day digital recipe hunter will flip for this prop block. Whether it's holding up a recipe card or a tablet, it's the perfect cook's companion.

APPLES TO APPLES

INGREDIENTS:

- 1 bottle sparkling apple cider
- 1 cup (240 mL) cranberry juice
- ½ cup (120 mL) orange juice

INSTRUCTIONS:

Stir all ingredients together, and serve. Use red and green cups topped with brown straws to really pull the theme together.

What You'll Need:

wood stain

3 ½ inch (9 centimeter) wood block

3 ½ inch piece of wood molding

medium plinth block

iron-on veneer tape

wood glue

1. With an adult's help, follow the instructions on the wood stain to stain the blocks. Let dry completely before continuing.
2. Decide where the wood block will connect to the plinth block and molding. Lightly mark those areas with a pencil.
3. Have an adult use a craft knife to cut the veneer tape into pieces. Use the tape to decorate the blocks as desired. Do not decorate inside the marked-off areas from step 2.
4. Place a piece of tinfoil over the tape-decorated blocks. Lightly press an iron on the cotton setting over the foil for 8 to 10 seconds. Repeat on the other side of the wood block, if necessary.
5. Connect the blocks and molding with wood glue. Let the glue dry at least 24 hours.

CRAFTING TIPS:

FOR BEST RESULTS, HAVE YOUR DESIGN FLOW FROM ONE BLOCK TO THE OTHER, RATHER THAN HAVING TWO DIFFERENT DESIGNS.

EXPERIMENT WITH A VARIETY OF WOOD STAINS AND VENEER TAPES. YOU COULD ALSO USE PAINT AND WASHI TAPE INSTEAD OF STAIN AND VENEER.

Sugary Snow Globes

You want to bring something special during holiday visits. Look like you went the extra mile with these easy snow globe cookies.

What You'll Need:

cookie cutters

1 teaspoon (5 milliliter) cream of tartar

1 teaspoon salt

1 teaspoon baking soda

5 cups (1.2 liters) flour

1 cup (240 mL) white sugar

1 cup powdered sugar

1 cup butter, softened

2 eggs

1 cup vegetable oil

1 tablespoon (15 mL) vanilla extract

1 teaspoon almond extract

clear hard candy, chopped into small pieces

sprinkles

white, brown, and red royal icing

fruit roll-up

1. Gather a snow globe-shaped cookie cutter and a smaller round cookie cutter. (Or use two round cookie cutters and a trapezoid-shaped cookie cutter.)
2. Stir together the cream of tartar, salt, baking soda, and flour in a large bowl.
3. In another bowl cream together the sugars and butter. Beat in the eggs, then the oil.
4. Slowly beat the flour mixture into the sugar mixture. Finally, mix in the vanilla and almond extracts.
5. Roll the dough out until it is ¼-inch (0.6 cm) thick. Cut out the snow globe and base. Press the two dough pieces together. Use the smaller cookie cutter to cut out the inside of the globe.

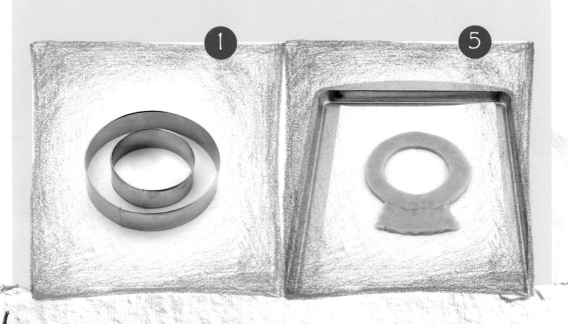

BAKING TIPS:

DISPLAY THE FINISHED COOKIES! USE ROYAL ICING TO ATTACH THE BASE OF THE COOKIE TO A GRAHAM CRACKER. COVER THE CRACKER WITH MELTED WHITE CHOCOLATE OR MORE ROYAL ICING AND A HANDFUL OF SPRINKLES OR SHREDDED COCONUT.

USE MORE ROYAL ICING TO WRITE NAMES ON EACH COOKIE. THEY CAN SERVE AS PERSONALIZED GIFTS OR AS PLACE CARDS.

CONTINUED ON NEXT PAGE

6. Fill the globe with chopped hard candy.
7. With an adult's help, bake cookies for 12 minutes, or until cookies are golden and candy is melted.
8. Decorate melted candy with small white sprinkles. Let the candy harden before moving the cookies onto your workspace.
9. Make and color the royal icing. Divide icing into three separate piping bags.
10. Color the entire outside of the globe with red icing. Start with the edges and then fill in the middle. Use a toothpick to spread the icing, if necessary.
11. Color the entire bottom of the globe with brown icing.

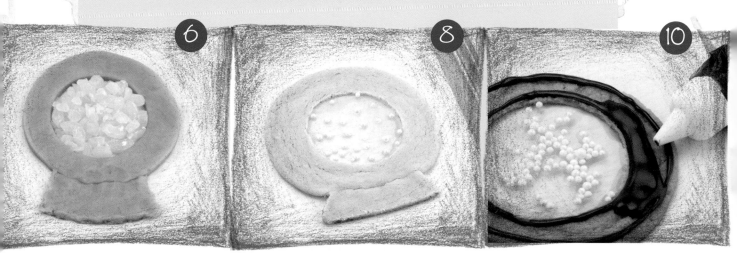

GIFTING TIPS:

Package cookies professionally by placing in cellophane bags. Use an old curling iron or flat iron to seal the bag closed.

Package unfrosted cookies with sealed piping bags of icing and small containers of sprinkles and candy for a DIY gift.

Use this recipe year-round. Hearts, stars, apples, pumpkins, shamrocks, flags, or even plain circles or squares make pretty cutout shapes.

12. Pipe a white snowman on the candy part of the globe. Let the icing harden for at least 30 minutes.
13. Give the snowman details such as eyes and buttons. Additional details you might want to add are a hat, arms, or pipe.
14. Cut the fruit roll-up into thin strips. Shape a strip around the snowman's neck for a scarf.

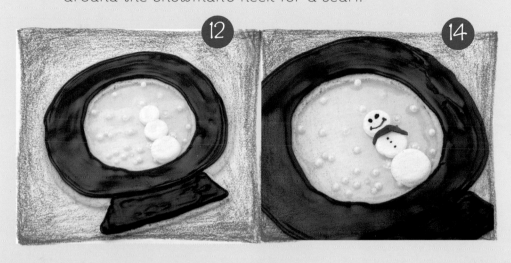

Royal Edge Icing

What You'll Need:

2 teaspoons (10 mL) meringue powder

2 tablespoons water

2 to 2 ½ cups (480 to 600 mL) confectioners' sugar

Instructions:

With a mixer on high, blend the ingredients together in a bowl for about four to five minutes. The icing is the right consistency when it forms little peaks that hold their shape.

Memory Box

Whether your VIP likes to travel or you've traveled together and want to collect your shared memories, this gift will be there to capture the moment.

What You'll Need:

hot glue and hot glue gun

two photo frames, one slightly smaller than the other

cardboard

photograph

scrapbook paper

rocks, miniature landscaping figures, or other trinkets

1. Remove the glass and backing from both frames.
2. Use hot glue to attach the smaller frame onto the larger frame.
3. Hold the smaller frame's glass in place with more hot glue.
4. Cut a piece of cardboard slightly smaller than your photo. Glue to the back of the photo.
5. Measure the length between the glass and the larger frame's backing. Cut small pieces of cardboard until you have a stack as thick as the length you measured. Glue all the cardboard pieces together. Then attach the stack of cardboard to the back of your photo. Arrange the photo in the center of the glass.
6. Glue scrapbook paper to the larger frame's backing.
7. Add sand and seashells to the shadow box. Replace the larger frame's backing.

CRAFTING TIP:

YOU CAN ADD ANYTHING YOU WANT TO THIS SHADOW BOX. TICKETS FROM ALL THE PLACES YOU AND YOUR VIP HAVE BEEN TO TOGETHER, TRINKETS, PHOTOGRAPHS, AND OTHER SPECIAL ITEMS YOU WANT TO DISPLAY ARE PERFECT SHADOW BOX ADDITIONS. IF YOU DON'T HAVE ANY SMALL ITEMS, DRILL A SMALL HOLE IN THE FRAME'S BACKING AND ADD HOLIDAY LIGHTS TO ILLUMINATE YOUR PHOTO.

Curious Candy

Mints are the perfect "just because" gift. Your recipient will think of you every time they need a minty treat.

What You'll Need:

ready-to-use gum paste

food-grade peppermint essential oil

gel food coloring

powdered sugar

very small round cookie cutter

1. Break off a handful of gum paste. Knead until it's soft and pliable.
2. Make a small well in the gum paste. Add food coloring and 5 drops of essential oil. Knead until the color is evenly distributed throughout the gum paste.
3. Lightly dust your work surface with powdered sugar. Pat or roll out the gum paste to about 1/8 of an inch thickness.
4. Use the cookie cutter to punch out shapes from the gum paste.
5. Once all your mints are cut out, toss them in some extra powdered sugar to make sure they don't stick together.
6. Spread mints out on a baking sheet and let them dry for 24 to 48 hours. They should be completely dry before packaging.

BAKING AND GIFTING TIPS:

YOU CAN FIND GUM PASTE IN THE CAKE DECORATING AISLE OF CRAFT STORES. FOOD-GRADE ESSENTIAL OIL CAN BE FOUND IN PHARMACIES AND AT HEALTH FOOD STORES.

FOR A CUTE PACKAGE, LAY A PIECE OF FABRIC PATTERN-SIDE DOWN ON YOUR WORK SURFACE. APPLY A THIN LAYER OF DECOUPAGE GLUE TO THE LID OF A METAL MINT TIN. LAY THE DECOUPAGED SIDE OF THE TIN ONTO THE FABRIC. FLIP IT OVER AND SMOOTH OUT ANY UNEVEN AREAS. ONCE THE GLUE IS DRY, USE SCISSORS TO TRIM OFF ANY EXCESS FABRIC.

MEASURE THE BOTTOM OF THE TIN THAT'S NOT COVERED BY THE TIN'S LID. CUT A PIECE OF FABRIC TO FIT. USE DECOUPAGE GLUE TO ATTACH THE FABRIC TO THE TIN. TRIM ANY FABRIC THAT HANGS OVER THE BOTTOM.

21

Totally Taped

Help your VIP get their thoughts in order with a coordinated set of stationery.

What You'll Need:

plain notebook

white acrylic paint

washi tape

scissors

1. Paint the front of the notebook with acrylic paint. This will help the washi tape stick better, and hide the notebook's color and design. Let dry completely. Repeat with the back side.
2. Starting in the center of the notebook, wrap washi tape at an angle all the way around the notebook. Secure the edges inside the notebook's cover.
3. Use scissors to trim the tape around the edge of the inside covers.

Washi Tape Pencils

What You'll Need:

pencils

white acrylic paint

washi tape

scissors

1. Paint the wooden part of the pencils with acrylic paint. Let dry completely.
2. Cut a piece of washi tape the same length as the pencil. Press tape onto the pencil. Repeat with a second strip, and a third strip if necessary. Trim ends with the scissors.

CRAFTING TIP:

Some brands of washi tape stick better than others. Thinner or waxy tapes don't stick as well. If your tape still doesn't stick well, try applying a little clear glue to seal the ends.

Style Statement

Giving jewelry as gifts doesn't have to be expensive! Metal washers, which are easily available at hardware stores, can be dressed up to become pretty presents.

What You'll Need:

20 large metal washers

alcohol ink in three colors

alcohol ink applicator

acrylic gel medium

ribbon

1. Lay washers flat on a newspaper-covered work surface.
2. Dab alcohol inks closely together onto applicator.
3. Use the applicator to sponge alcohol ink all over the washers. Let dry overnight.
4. Turn washers over; repeat steps 2-3.
5. Seal with acrylic gel medium. This will seal the ink's color.
6. Run the ribbon through a washer. Then run the ribbon through a second washer.
7. Thread the end of the ribbon back through the first washer. Pull tight. The washers should overlap each other now.
8. Repeat step 7 until all the washers are used. Tie the ribbon to make a necklace.

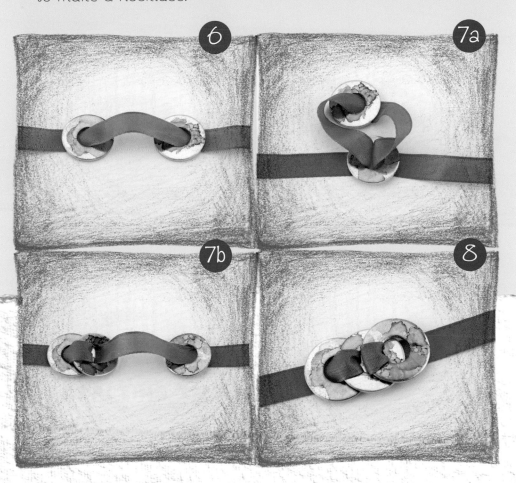

CRAFTING TIPS:

ALCOHOL INK IS A FAST-DRYING TRANSLUCENT DYE THAT CREATES A GLOSSY, POLISHED FINISH. UNLIKE ACRYLIC PAINT, IT CAN BE USED ON METAL WITHOUT PRIMER.

USE THE REST OF YOUR ALCOHOL INK ON CLEAR ORNAMENTS OR OTHER GLASS OBJECTS, COASTERS, OR POLYMER CLAY. YOU CAN ALSO USE IT FOR RUBBER STAMPING PROJECTS AND SCRAPBOOKING.

Fold 1t, Hold 1t

Make a simple gift card look like a million bucks with just a piece of paper and a few folds.

1. Place paper color-side down on your work station. Fold in half vertically. Unfold.
2. Fold the sides of the paper in so the edges meet in the center. Unfold.
3. Fold the bottom right corner in so it lines up with the nearest crease line. Repeat for all four corners.
4. Fold the sides of the paper in so the edges meet in the center.
5. Flip paper over. Fold the top of the paper down and crease at the top of the white triangle.
6. Repeat with the bottom of the paper. The edges of the colored triangles should slightly overlap.
7. Insert gift card. Fold paper in half and seal with glue dot.

GIFTING TIPS:

THIS MINI WALLET HOLDS MORE THAN GIFT CARDS! SLIP A TEA BAG IN ONE POCKET AND A SUGAR PACKET IN THE OTHER. OR ADD A SMALL PACKAGE OF CANDY FOR AN AFTERNOON TREAT. PHOTOS, MESSAGES, AND DIY GIFT CERTIFICATES ARE THE PERFECT SIZE TOO.

MAKE THE WALLET AS BIG OR AS SMALL AS YOU NEED. OLD CALENDAR PAGES, SCRAPBOOK PAPER, GRAPH PAPER, AND BUTCHER PAPER ARE SOME PLUS-SIZE PAGE IDEAS.

Tick Tock

Remind the hardest worker in your life that sometimes it's nice to slow down. They'll be sure to check the time often with a colorful clock nearby.

What You'll Need:

clock

spray paint

scrapbooking paper

scrapbooking numbers

1. Take the clock apart. You should have the frame, plastic cover, clock hands, battery pack, and paper dial.
2. Spread newspapers on a work surface in a well-ventilated area. Use spray paint to color the clock frame. Let dry completely. Repeat, if a second coat is desired.
3. Use the dial to trace and cut out a piece of scrapbook paper.
4. Glue the scrapbooking numbers onto your new dial.
5. Poke the clock hands through the center of the dial.
6. Put the clock back together.

CRAFTING TIPS:

INSTEAD OF SCRAPBOOK PAPER, USE A PHOTOGRAPH TO MAKE YOUR CLOCK MORE PERSONAL. OR USE SMALL PHOTOGRAPHS INSTEAD OF NUMBERS.

ANYTHING CAN BE A CLOCK! WOODEN PLAQUES, ART CANVASES, PICTURE FRAMES, OLD BOOKS, BICYCLE RIMS, AND CORKBOARD ARE ALL IDEAS FOR A DIY CLOCK. AS LONG AS YOU CAN DRILL A HOLE FOR THE WATCH HANDS, YOU CAN MAKE IT INTO A CLOCK! RECYCLE THE BATTERY PACK AND HANDS FROM AN INEXPENSIVE CLOCK, OR BUY A CLOCK KIT.

Memorable Mittens

Turn a treasured sweater into an accessory you'll always have "on hand" as a reminder.

What You'll Need:

knit sweater

chalk

needle and thread

GIFTING TIP:

MITTENS MAKE GREAT PACKAGING FOR GIFTS! FILL THEM WITH CANDY, COCOA MIX, SMALL ORNAMENTS, AND OTHER TINY TRINKETS.

1. Turn the sweater inside out. Lay your hand along the bottom hem line of the sweater, with your thumb slightly out to the side. The hem line will be the mitten cuff. Use chalk to trace your hand. Add ½ inch (1.2 cm) all the way around to allow for the seams.
2. Repeat step 1 with your opposite hand.
3. Make loose stitches around the mitten shapes. This will prevent the mitten from fraying when you cut.
4. Cut out the mitten shapes and stack them on top of each other. Sew along the outside of the mitten, leaving the bottom open.
5. Turn the mitten inside out.
6. Repeat steps 1-5 for a second mitten.

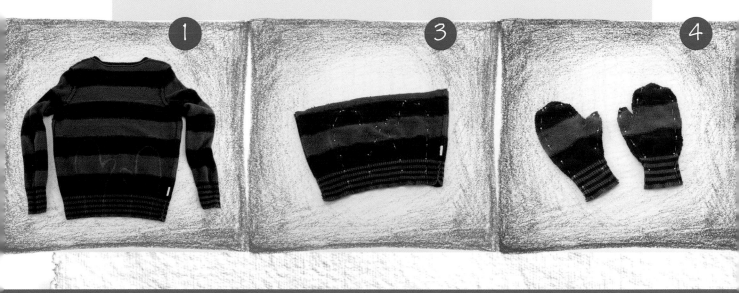

Sewing by Hand:

Slide the thread through the eye of the needle. Tie the end of the thread into a knot. Poke the needle through the underside of the fabric. Pull the thread through the fabric to the knotted end. Poke your needle back through the fabric and up again to make a stitch.

Continue weaving the needle in and out of the fabric, making small stitches in a straight line. When you are finished sewing, make a loose stitch. Thread the needle through the loop and pull tight. Cut off remaining thread.

Read More:

Formaro, Amanda. *Paper Fun Mania*. White Plains, N.Y.: Studio Fun International, Inc., 2014.

Laz, Ashley Ann. *Totally Washi!* Avon, Mass.: Adams, 20014.

Turnbull, Stephanie. *Cards and Gifts: Style Secrets for Girls*. Girl Talk. Mankato, Minn.: Smart Apple Media, 2014.

Titles in this series: